Mastery of money for parents
A Parent's Guide to Mastering Money

By

William K. Lozano

Table of contents

INTRODUCTION

As parents, we often find ourselves navigating the complex world of personal finance, both for ourselves and for our children. Teaching our children about money is an essential aspect of their overall education and development, preparing them for a financially responsible future. However, in order to guide our children effectively, it is crucial that we first attain mastery over our own relationship with money.

The mastery of money encompasses various skills and principles that enable us to make informed financial decisions, manage our resources effectively, and build a stable financial foundation for our families. It involves understanding concepts such as budgeting, saving, investing, and debt management, and applying them in our everyday lives.

By mastering money, parents can set a positive example for their children, instilling in them healthy financial habits and attitudes from an early age. When children witness responsible money management firsthand, they are more likely to develop a strong sense of financial literacy and make sound financial choices as they grow older.

Moreover, mastering money as parents allows us to create a nurturing and financially secure environment for our children. It empowers us to provide for their needs, plan for their future, and teach them the value of money and the importance of delayed gratification. When we have a solid understanding of our own financial situation, we can make thoughtful decisions that prioritize our family's well-being and long-term goals.

In this guide on the mastery of money for parents, we will explore various aspects of personal finance and provide practical tips and strategies to help you enhance your financial literacy and take control of your family's financial well-being. From setting up a budget and managing expenses to teaching your children about money and planning for their education, we will cover a range of topics that are relevant to parents seeking to master their finances.

Remember, the journey to financial mastery is an ongoing process, and it requires patience, discipline, and a willingness to learn. By embarking on this journey, not only will you enhance your own financial situation, but you will also equip your children with invaluable life skills that will serve them well throughout their lives.

So, let's dive in and begin our exploration of the mastery of money for parents, taking a proactive step toward a brighter financial future for you and your family.

Chapter 1

Budgeting and financial plannings

Budgeting is the process of creating a plan for your income and expenses. It involves allocating funds to various categories such as housing, transportation, groceries, entertainment, savings, and more. The primary objective of budgeting is to ensure that you are spending your money wisely and in line with your financial goals.

Why Financial Literacy Matters for Parents:
In an increasingly complex and financially-driven world, the need for financial literacy has never been greater. Among those who have a crucial role to play in shaping the financial well-being of future generations, parents stand at the forefront. By equipping themselves with financial knowledge and skills, parents can make informed decisions, teach their children valuable lessons about money management, and set them up for a lifetime of

financial success. This article explores why financial literacy matters for parents and highlights the benefits it brings to both parents and their children.

Leading by Example

Parents serve as the primary role models for their children, and their attitudes and behaviors towards money significantly influence their offspring's financial habits. By demonstrating responsible financial practices, such as budgeting, saving, and investing wisely, parents can instill positive money values in their children. When parents exhibit financial literacy, children are more likely to emulate those habits and develop a healthy relationship with money from an early age.

Making Informed Financial Decisions

Financial literacy empowers parents to make sound financial decisions that affect their family's well-being. From creating a realistic budget to managing debt effectively, understanding concepts like interest rates, inflation, and investment strategies enables parents to navigate the complexities of personal finance confidently. With financial literacy, parents can make informed choices about savings plans, insurance coverage, and long-term investments, ensuring their family's financial security.

Teaching Financial Responsibility
Children begin learning about money long before they have their own income. By teaching children about basic financial concepts and practices, parents can impart valuable life skills and prepare them for financial independence. Financially literate parents can introduce age-appropriate lessons, such as budgeting, distinguishing needs from wants, and the importance of saving for the future. These lessons set the foundation for responsible financial behavior, enabling children to make informed decisions as they grow older.

Fostering Financial Confidence

Financial literacy equips parents with the knowledge to navigate financial challenges and unexpected circumstances with confidence. Understanding concepts like insurance, taxes, and investment options provides a sense of control over one's financial well-being. This confidence is essential for parents in planning for their family's future, setting financial goals, and managing financial emergencies. By addressing these matters proactively, parents can alleviate financial stress and create a stable environment for their children.

Preparing for Higher Education Costs

The cost of higher education continues to rise, placing a significant financial burden on families. However, financially literate parents can prepare for these expenses by exploring savings options, such as 529 plans or other education savings accounts, and understanding student loans and financial aid programs. By effectively managing these costs and exploring available resources, parents can help alleviate the financial strain associated with their children's educational pursuits.

Navigating Technological Advancements
In today's digital era, financial transactions are increasingly conducted online, and new financial technologies emerge regularly. Parents with financial literacy are better equipped to navigate these advancements, ensuring their family's financial security. Understanding concepts like online banking, mobile payments, and digital identity theft protection helps parents safeguard their financial information and adapt to the changing landscape of financial services.

The Impact of Financial Literacy on Children
Establishing Healthy Money Habits:
Financial literacy empowers children with essential money management skills, allowing them to develop healthy financial habits from a young age.

Teaching children about budgeting, saving, and spending responsibly helps them understand the value of money and the importance of setting financial goals. By instilling these habits early on, children can avoid falling into the trap of overspending, debt, and poor financial choices in their adult lives.

Building Confidence and Independence:
Financial literacy equips children with the confidence and independence to make sound financial decisions. When children understand basic financial concepts, such as earning, budgeting, and investing, they become active participants in their financial well-being. This knowledge helps them develop critical thinking skills, enabling them to evaluate financial opportunities and make informed choices. As a result, children grow into financially responsible adults capable of managing their finances effectively.

Fostering Entrepreneurial Spirit:
Financial literacy encourages an entrepreneurial mindset in children. By teaching them about concepts such as income generation, profit, and investment, children gain a deeper understanding of the value of money and the potential it holds. This knowledge sparks creativity, innovation, and the desire to explore business opportunities. With a solid financial foundation, children are more likely to pursue entrepreneurial ventures and contribute to economic growth and innovation in the future.

Promoting Future Financial Stability:
A lack of financial literacy can have long-lasting consequences on an individual's financial stability. Without a basic understanding of financial concepts, individuals are more susceptible to falling into debt, making poor investment decisions, and experiencing financial hardships. By educating children about personal finance, the power of saving, and the importance of making informed

decisions, we equip them with the tools they need to build a secure financial future. Financially literate children are more likely to achieve financial independence, save for emergencies, and plan for retirement effectively.

Encouraging Responsible Citizenship:
Financial literacy also plays a crucial role in fostering responsible citizenship. By understanding the economic principles that drive societies, children gain insights into how their financial decisions can impact not only their lives but also the broader community. Financially literate individuals are more likely to make sustainable choices, support local businesses, contribute to charitable causes, and participate actively in the economy. By instilling a sense of financial responsibility and ethical decision-making, we nurture citizens who can positively contribute to society.

Teaching parents how create and stick to budget:
Assessing Current Financial Situation

The first step in creating a successful budget is to assess your current financial situation. Gather all relevant financial documents, including income statements, bills, and bank statements. Take note of your monthly income, fixed expenses (such as rent/mortgage, utilities, and debt payments), and variable expenses (such as groceries, transportation, and entertainment).

Setting Financial Goals

Setting clear financial goals is crucial to stay motivated and focused on your budgeting journey. Determine both short-term and long-term goals, such as saving for emergencies, education, retirement, or a family vacation. These goals will guide your budgeting decisions and help you prioritize expenses accordingly.

Creating a Realistic Budget

Based on your assessment and financial goals, it's time to create a budget. Start by listing all your sources of income and deducting fixed expenses. Allocate a portion of your income for savings and debt repayments. For variable expenses, establish spending limits in categories such as groceries, entertainment, and clothing.

Ensure that your budget is realistic and flexible. It should strike a balance between meeting your family's needs and allowing for occasional indulgences. Remember to account for irregular expenses, such as annual insurance premiums or holiday gifts, by setting aside a small amount each month to avoid sudden financial strain.

Tracking and Monitoring Expenses

Tracking your expenses is essential to stay accountable and ensure that you're sticking to your budget. Use tools like smartphone apps or budgeting software to record and categorize expenses. Regularly review your spending patterns to identify areas where you can cut back and make adjustments if necessary.

Encouraging Open Communication

Budgeting is a family affair, and it's crucial to involve your spouse and children in the process. Discuss financial goals with your family and explain the importance of budgeting. Encourage open communication about financial matters, fostering an environment where everyone understands the need for financial discipline and makes a collective effort to stick to the budget.

Seeking Savings Opportunities

Implementing smart savings strategies can significantly impact your financial well-being. Look for opportunities to reduce expenses, such as cutting back on dining out, entertainment subscriptions, or unnecessary purchases. Consider utilizing coupons, shopping during sales, or buying in bulk to save money on groceries. Explore options to save on utilities by conserving energy or switching to more cost-effective plans.

Addressing Debt

Debt can impede financial progress, so it's crucial to address it strategically. Allocate a portion of your budget towards debt repayments, focusing on high-interest obligations first. Consider debt consolidation or negotiation options to lower interest rates or monthly payments. Seek professional advice if needed, such as credit counseling services, to create an effective debt repayment plan.

Building an Emergency Fund

Life is unpredictable, and unexpected expenses can disrupt even the most well-planned budget. Therefore, it's essential to build an emergency fund to handle unforeseen circumstances. Allocate a percentage of your income towards this fund, gradually accumulating three to six months' worth of living expenses. This safety net will provide peace of mind and protect your budget from unexpected shocks.

Celebrating Milestones

Achieving financial milestones is worth celebrating and can motivate you to stick to your budget. Whether it's paying off a debt, reaching a savings goal, or consistently adhering to your budget for a specific period, acknowledge these achievements. Reward yourself and your family with a small treat or a simple celebration. It will reinforce the value of budgeting and boost morale to continue on your financial journey.

Chapter 2

Estate management and wills

Estate management and wills are two crucial aspects of planning for the future and safeguarding your assets. They play a vital role in ensuring that your wishes are carried out and your loved ones are taken care of when you're no longer around. Let's delve into what estate management and wills entail and why they are essential.

Estate management refers to the overall administration and control of an individual's assets, properties, and financial affairs during their lifetime and after their passing. It involves organizing, protecting, and distributing assets in a way that aligns with the owner's intentions and objectives. Estate management is not only about wealthy individuals; it applies to people from all walks of life who have assets, no matter how big or small.

A will, on the other hand, is a legal document that outlines how a person's assets and possessions should be distributed after their death. It enables you to specify beneficiaries, designate guardians for minor children, and even provide instructions on matters like funeral arrangements. Wills are highly customizable and allow you to ensure that your assets are divided according to your wishes, rather than being subject to default laws or court decisions.

Having an estate management plan and a will in place offers numerous benefits. Firstly, it allows you to have control over what happens to your assets, ensuring that they are passed on to the individuals or charitable causes you care about. Without a will, the laws of intestacy will dictate how your estate is distributed, which may not align with your preferences.

Secondly, estate management and wills help minimize the potential for family disputes and conflicts. By clearly outlining your wishes and intentions, you reduce the chances of disagreements among family members regarding asset distribution. This can alleviate stress and maintain harmony among your loved ones during an already challenging time.

Additionally, estate management and wills can help reduce taxes and expenses associated with estate administration. By engaging in strategic planning, you can take advantage of tax-saving opportunities and minimize the financial burden on your beneficiaries. Proper estate management can also address issues such as creditor claims, outstanding debts, and funeral expenses, ensuring that your loved ones are not burdened with these responsibilities.

It is important to regularly review and update your estate management plan and will to reflect any changes in your life circumstances or financial situation. Significant life events like marriage, divorce, the birth of a child, or the acquisition of new assets should prompt a review of your plan to ensure its accuracy and alignment with your current wishes.

Seeking professional advice from an estate planning attorney or financial advisor is highly recommended when establishing your estate management plan and drafting a will. These experts can guide you through the legal intricacies and help you make informed decisions that protect your assets and best serve your loved ones.

Parenting is an exhilarating journey filled with joy, love, and countless memorable moments. However, it's also a responsibility that comes with its fair share of challenges and uncertainties. While we may have a general plan in mind for raising our children, life often throws unexpected curveballs our way. That's why it's crucial for parents to embrace the concept of planning for the unexpected. By doing so, they can navigate the unknown with confidence and ensure the well-being of their families.

Build a Strong Support Network: One of the most valuable assets parents can have is a reliable support network. Cultivate relationships with friends, family members, and other parents who can offer guidance, assistance, and emotional support when needed. A strong support system can provide a crucial safety net during unexpected situations, helping to alleviate stress and provide practical help.

Planning for unexpected
Financial Preparedness: As parents, it's essential to establish a solid financial plan. Save for emergencies, create a budget, and consider obtaining life insurance or disability insurance to protect your

family's financial future. Having a financial safety net will provide peace of mind during unexpected events and ensure that you can handle any financial challenges that may arise.

Prioritize Communication: Open and effective communication within the family is vital, especially when faced with unexpected situations. Encourage your children to express their thoughts and concerns openly, creating an atmosphere of trust and support. Additionally, maintain open lines of communication with your partner to ensure that you are on the same page when it comes to decision-making during challenging times.

Practice Flexibility: Life rarely goes according to plan, and being a parent is no exception. Embracing flexibility is key to adapting to unexpected situations. Accept that there may be detours along the parenting journey and be prepared to adjust your expectations and plans accordingly. By cultivating a flexible mindset, you'll be better equipped to handle whatever comes your way.

Take Care of Yourself: Parenting can be demanding, both physically and emotionally. It's crucial to prioritize self-care and maintain your well-being. Ensure you're getting enough rest, eating a balanced diet, and engaging in activities that recharge you. By taking care of yourself, you'll be better equipped to handle unexpected challenges and be a positive role model for your children.

Continual Learning: Parenting is a constant learning process. Stay informed about child development, safety measures, and best practices in parenting. This knowledge will empower you to make informed decisions and navigate unexpected situations more effectively. Attend parenting workshops, read books or articles, and consult professionals when needed.

Embrace Resilience: Resilience is a valuable trait for parents facing the unexpected. Life may present unexpected health issues, accidents, or changes in circumstances, but by embracing resilience, you can bounce back stronger. Cultivate a positive mindset, seek support when needed, and maintain perspective during challenging times. Remember that setbacks are temporary, and you have the strength to overcome them.

In the unpredictable journey of parenthood, planning for the unexpected is a crucial aspect of responsible parenting. By building a strong support network, being financially prepared, prioritizing communication, practicing flexibility, taking care of yourself, continually learning, and embracing resilience, parents can navigate the unknown with confidence and ensure a secure and nurturing environment for their children. Remember, it's not about avoiding challenges but rather being prepared to face them head-on and emerge stronger as a family.

Creating a Will and Estate Plan.

knowing that your wishes will be carried out and your children will be taken care of in the event of unforeseen circumstances.

Here are some key points to consider as you embark on the process of creating your will and estate plan:

Appointment of Guardians: One of the most important decisions you will make is appointing a guardian for your minor children. This individual will assume responsibility for their care and upbringing if both parents pass away. Choose someone who shares your values, is capable of taking on this responsibility, and is willing to fulfill this role.

Asset Distribution: Decide how you want your assets to be distributed among your children or other beneficiaries. Consider their financial needs, age, and ability to manage the inheritance. You may want to set up a trust to protect their assets until they reach a certain age or achieve specific milestones.

Healthcare and Financial Power of Attorney: Designate someone you trust to make medical and financial decisions on your behalf if you become incapacitated. This individual, known as the power of attorney, should understand your wishes and be capable of acting in your best interest.

Executor: Select an executor who will be responsible for administering your estate according to your wishes. This person will ensure that your debts are paid, assets are distributed, and legal matters are handled appropriately. Choose someone who is organized, trustworthy, and capable of fulfilling this role.

Digital Assets: In today's digital age, it's crucial to consider your digital assets such as online accounts, social media profiles, and cryptocurrencies. Specify how you want these assets to be handled, whether you want them to be deleted, transferred, or managed by someone else.

Regularly Review and Update: It's essential to review your will and estate plan periodically to ensure they align with your current circumstances. Major life events such as the birth of a child, divorce, or the death of a beneficiary may require updates to your documents.

Seek Professional Assistance: While it is possible to create a basic will and estate plan on your own, it is highly recommended to consult with an attorney who specializes in estate planning. They can provide legal advice, help navigate complex tax laws, and ensure that your documents are valid and enforceable.

Creating a will and estate plan is an act of love and responsibility towards your children. It provides them with a clear roadmap and protection in the event of the unexpected. By taking these steps, you are securing their future and giving yourself peace of mind.

Guidance and trust

As parents, one of our primary concerns is ensuring the well-being and security of our children. While we may not like to dwell on the possibility of unforeseen circumstances, it is crucial to have a plan in place for the care and financial stability of our minor children. Guardianship and trusts are two essential tools that can provide peace of mind and secure a brighter future for our little ones.

Guardianship is a legal arrangement where a designated person, known as the guardian, assumes the responsibility of caring for a minor child in the event that the child's parents are unable to do so. It is crucial to name a guardian in your will or establish guardianship through a legal process, as it ensures that your child will be cared for by someone you trust and who shares your values.

Selecting the right guardian requires thoughtful consideration. Take into account factors such as the person's age, their relationship with your child, their values, and their ability to provide a stable and loving environment. Engage in open discussions with potential guardians to ensure they are willing to accept the responsibility and understand your wishes regarding your child's upbringing.

Trusts

While guardianship focuses on the care and upbringing of your children, trusts are an effective means to manage and protect their financial well-being. A trust is a legal entity that holds and manages assets for the benefit of the beneficiaries, in this case, your minor children. By establishing a trust, you can ensure that your children's financial needs are met even if you are no longer there to provide for them directly.

There are different types of trusts that can be used for the benefit of minor children. One common option is a testamentary trust, which is established through a will and takes effect upon your passing. This trust allows you to designate a trustee who will manage the assets on behalf of your children until they reach a specified age or milestone, such as turning 18 or completing their education.

Another option is a living trust, also known as an inter vivos trust, which is created during your lifetime. By transferring assets into the trust, you retain control over the management of those assets until you are unable to do so. In the event of your incapacity or death, a designated trustee steps in to manage the trust for the benefit of your children according to the instructions you have outlined.

Trusts offer several benefits beyond financial security. They can provide protection from creditors, ensure that the assets are used for specific purposes (such as education or healthcare), and allow for more control over the distribution of assets. Additionally, trusts can help minimize estate taxes and avoid the costly and time-consuming probate process.

The Importance of Professional Guidance
Establishing guardianship and trusts for minor children is a complex legal process that requires careful consideration and attention to detail. It is advisable to seek professional guidance from an estate planning attorney who specializes in these matters. An attorney can help you navigate the legal requirements, explain the available options, and ensure that your wishes are accurately reflected in legally binding documents.

Regular Review and Updates

Guardianship and trust arrangements should not be set in stone. It is crucial to review and update these documents regularly to reflect changes in your family circumstances, financial situation, or the availability and suitability of potential guardians. Births, deaths, divorces, and changes in your financial status should prompt a review of your plans to ensure they remain aligned with your current wishes and circumstances.

Communication is Key

Lastly, open and honest communication with the chosen guardian(s) and trustee(s) is essential. Ensure that the individuals you have designated understand their roles and responsibilities, and keep them informed about your intentions and any changes you make to your plans over time. This clarity and transparency can help avoid confusion or disputes in the future and provide a smooth transition for your children in case the need for guardianship or trust arises.

Chapter 3

Saving and investing

Saving and investing are crucial financial practices that play a significant role in securing your future and achieving long-term financial goals. Here are several reasons why saving and investing are important:

Financial Security: Saving money provides a safety net for unexpected expenses, emergencies, or unforeseen circumstances. Having a financial cushion helps you avoid falling into debt or relying on high-interest loans, ensuring greater stability and peace of mind.

Achieving Goals: Saving and investing allow you to work towards specific goals, such as buying a home, starting a business, funding education, or planning for retirement. By regularly setting aside money and making smart investment choices, you increase your chances of realizing these aspirations.

Beat Inflation: Inflation is the gradual increase in the cost of goods and services over time. Saving money without considering inflation means its purchasing power decreases. Investing allows your money to grow at a rate that keeps up with or surpasses inflation, preserving and enhancing your wealth.

Building Wealth: Investing offers the potential for significant wealth accumulation. By putting your money to work through various investment vehicles like stocks, bonds, real estate, or mutual funds, you have the opportunity to grow your savings exponentially over time and generate passive income.

Retirement Planning: Saving and investing are critical components of retirement planning. Relying solely on government pensions or social security may not be sufficient to maintain your desired lifestyle during retirement. By saving and investing early, you can take advantage of compound interest and build a substantial retirement nest egg.

Financial Independence: Saving and investing allow you to achieve financial independence, where your investments generate enough income to cover your expenses without relying on a regular job. This financial freedom provides flexibility and the ability to pursue your passions, take risks, or retire early.

Capitalizing on Opportunities: Having savings and investment capital puts you in a position to seize opportunities as they arise. Whether it's starting a business, investing in a promising venture, or taking advantage of a favorable market condition, having financial resources enables you to capitalize on such situations.

Diversification: Investing in a diverse range of assets spreads your risk and reduces the impact of market fluctuations. By diversifying your investment portfolio, you minimize the likelihood of significant losses and increase the potential for consistent returns.

Generational Wealth: Saving and investing can create a legacy of financial well-being for future generations. By making wise investment decisions, you can build wealth that can be passed down to your children or beneficiaries, providing them with greater opportunities and security.

In summary, saving and investing are essential for building financial security, achieving goals, beating inflation, building wealth, planning for retirement, attaining financial independence, capitalizing on opportunities, diversifying risk, and creating generational wealth.

Investing for the future is of significant importance for several reasons. Here are some key reasons why investing is crucial for securing your financial future:

Wealth accumulation: Investing allows you to grow your wealth over time. By putting your money to work in different asset classes such as stocks, bonds, real estate, or mutual funds, you have the potential to earn returns that outpace inflation. This helps you build a nest egg and achieve long-term financial goals such as retirement or funding your children's education.

Inflation protection: Inflation erodes the purchasing power of money over time. By investing, you can aim to earn returns that exceed the inflation rate. This enables your investments to maintain or increase their value over the long run, protecting your purchasing power and ensuring you can meet future financial needs.

Retirement planning: Investing early and consistently is crucial for retirement planning. With the decline of traditional pension plans and the uncertainty surrounding government-funded retirement benefits, it's essential to take responsibility for your own retirement savings. By investing in retirement accounts like 401(k)s or IRAs, you can harness the power of compounding and potentially achieve a comfortable retirement lifestyle.

Achieving financial goals: Investing provides you with the opportunity to achieve various financial goals, such as buying a house, starting a business, or funding a dream vacation. By allocating funds to different investment vehicles based on your risk tolerance and time horizon, you can work towards specific objectives and increase your chances of reaching them.

Diversification and risk management: Investing allows you to diversify your assets across different investments, spreading your risk. A well-diversified portfolio can help mitigate the impact of any single investment's poor performance. By investing in a mix of asset classes, industries, and geographical regions, you can reduce the risk associated with individual investments and increase the likelihood of long-term success.

Taking advantage of compounding: Compound interest is the concept of earning returns on your original investment and any accumulated earnings. By investing early and allowing your investments to compound over time, you can potentially benefit from exponential growth. The longer your money remains invested, the greater the impact of compounding, and the more significant your potential returns.

Beat inflation and taxes: Keeping your money in low-interest savings accounts or under the mattress may not be sufficient to keep pace with inflation. Investing in assets with the potential for growth allows you to generate returns that exceed inflation, helping you preserve and grow your wealth. Additionally, certain investment vehicles offer tax advantages, such as retirement accounts or tax-efficient funds, which can optimize your after-tax returns.

It's important to note that investing involves risks, including the potential loss of principal. It's advisable to conduct thorough research, diversify your investments, and consider seeking professional advice to align your investment strategy with your financial goals, risk tolerance, and time horizon.

Chapter 4

Building and maintaining good credit

Building and maintaining good credit is an essential financial goal for individuals and businesses alike. A solid credit history opens up numerous opportunities, from obtaining loans and credit cards with favorable terms to securing better insurance rates and even enhancing job prospects. It is a long-term process that requires discipline, responsibility, and a commitment to financial well-being. In this article, we will explore the key steps involved in building and maintaining good credit.

The first step towards establishing good credit is to understand where you currently stand. Obtain copies of your credit reports from the major credit bureaus - Equifax, Experian, and TransUnion - and review them carefully. Check for any errors, such as incorrect personal information or inaccurate account details. If you spot any discrepancies, report them immediately to the respective credit bureaus to have them corrected.

Once you have a clear picture of your credit history, it's time to start building positive credit. The most important factor in building good credit is making timely payments. Pay all your bills, including credit card bills, loan installments, and utility bills, on time each month. Late payments can have a significant negative impact on your credit score, so it's crucial to stay organized and prioritize your financial obligations.

Another key element in building good credit is maintaining a low credit utilization ratio. This ratio reflects the amount of credit you are using compared to the total credit available to you. To keep your credit utilization ratio low, aim to use no more than 30% of your available credit. For example, if you have a credit card with a $1,000 limit, try to keep your balance below $300. High credit utilization can signal to lenders that you may be relying too heavily on credit and may have difficulty repaying your debts.

Diversifying your credit portfolio can also strengthen your creditworthiness. Having a mix of different types of credit, such as credit cards, auto loans, and mortgages, demonstrates your ability to handle different forms of debt responsibly. However, be cautious and only take on credit that you genuinely need and can manage effectively.

Regularly monitoring your credit is an essential part of maintaining good credit. Stay vigilant by reviewing your credit reports periodically and checking for any suspicious activity or unauthorized accounts. If you notice anything unusual, report it immediately to the credit bureaus and the relevant financial institutions.

be patient and stay committed to your financial goals. Building good credit takes time and consistent effort. Avoid unnecessary credit inquiries and focus on responsible credit management. Over time, your credit score will improve, providing you with greater financial opportunities.

building and maintaining good credit is a journey that requires discipline and responsibility. By making timely payments, keeping your credit utilization low, diversifying your credit portfolio, and regularly monitoring your credit, you can establish a solid credit history. Remember, good credit opens doors to better financial options and can contribute to your long-term financial success.

The importance of a credit score cannot be overstated in today's financial landscape. A credit score is a numerical representation of an individual's creditworthiness, and it plays a crucial role in determining their eligibility for loans, credit cards, mortgages, and other financial products. It is essentially a measure of how responsible a person is with managing their debt and fulfilling their financial obligations.

Here are some key reasons why a credit score is important:

Loan Eligibility: Lenders, such as banks and financial institutions, heavily rely on credit scores to assess the risk associated with lending money to individuals. A high credit score indicates a low level of risk, making it easier for individuals to qualify for loans and obtain favorable interest rates and terms. On the other hand, a poor credit score can lead to loan rejections or higher interest rates, making borrowing more expensive and difficult.

Interest Rates: A good credit score can significantly impact the interest rates offered by lenders. Those with excellent credit scores are more likely to secure loans or credit cards with lower interest rates, saving them a substantial amount of money in interest payments over time. Conversely, individuals with lower credit scores may be subject to higher interest rates, increasing the cost of borrowing.

Access to Credit: A solid credit score opens doors to various credit opportunities. It enables individuals to access credit cards, lines of credit, and other forms of financing that can be beneficial for emergencies, building a business, or making significant purchases. Credit cards, for example, provide convenience, security, and a means to build credit history when used responsibly.

Housing and Rental Applications: Landlords and property management companies often run credit checks when evaluating rental applications. A good credit score demonstrates financial responsibility and a lower likelihood of defaulting on rent payments. It can increase the chances of securing a desirable rental property and negotiating more favorable lease terms.

Employment Opportunities: Certain employers, particularly those in the financial industry or positions that involve handling sensitive financial information, may consider credit scores as part of their hiring process. A good credit score can be seen as a reflection of an individual's reliability, responsibility, and ability to manage finances, making them more appealing to potential employers.

Insurance Premiums: Insurance companies may use credit scores to assess risk and determine insurance premiums for auto, home, or other types of insurance policies. Studies have shown that individuals with lower credit scores are more likely to file insurance claims, leading to higher premiums for those individuals. Maintaining a good credit score can help individuals secure more affordable insurance rates.

Negotiating Power: A strong credit score empowers individuals to negotiate better terms and conditions when dealing with lenders or financial institutions. With a good credit history, individuals can leverage their creditworthiness to request lower interest rates, higher credit limits, or more favorable repayment terms, giving them greater control over their financial options.

 a credit score is a vital financial tool that influences an individual's access to credit, loan eligibility, interest rates, housing opportunities, insurance premiums, and even employment prospects. Maintaining a good credit score requires responsible financial habits, such as making timely bill payments, keeping credit utilization low, and managing debt effectively. By doing so, individuals can reap the benefits of a positive credit history and secure a solid foundation for their financial well-being.

Establishing and Improving Your Credit:
Your credit score plays a vital role in your financial life. Whether you're applying for a loan, renting an apartment, or even securing a job, your creditworthiness is often evaluated to determine your reliability and trustworthiness as a borrower. Establishing and improving your credit is essential for achieving financial goals and building a strong foundation for your future. In this article, we will explore key steps and strategies to help you navigate the world of credit.

Understand the Basics of Credit:
Before diving into credit-building techniques, it's crucial to grasp the fundamentals. Credit is a measure of your ability to borrow money and repay it over time. It is tracked by credit bureaus, which compile information from various sources, such as

lenders and creditors, to generate your credit report and calculate your credit score. Your credit score, usually ranging from 300 to 850, reflects your creditworthiness. Higher scores indicate lower risk, making it easier to access loans and secure favorable interest rates.

Start with the Essentials: Establishing Credit:
If you're new to the credit world, building credit from scratch is the first step. Consider the following options to kickstart your credit journey:

a. Apply for a secured credit card: Secured credit cards require a cash deposit that serves as collateral. They offer a great starting point for building credit as they are often available to individuals with limited or no credit history.

b. Become an authorized user: Ask a family member or a close friend with a good credit history to add you as an authorized user on one of their credit cards. This can help you benefit from their positive credit history and establish your own credit.

c. Obtain a credit-builder loan: Some financial institutions offer credit-builder loans designed specifically for individuals looking to establish credit. These loans hold the borrowed funds in an account while you make monthly payments, gradually building credit.

Make Timely Payments:
Payment history is a crucial factor in determining your credit score, accounting for a significant portion of its calculation. Always pay your bills on time, including credit card payments, loans, utilities, and any other recurring expenses. Late payments can have a detrimental impact on your credit score, so it's vital to establish a habit of punctual payments.

Keep Credit Utilization Low:

Credit utilization refers to the percentage of available credit you're currently using. It is recommended to keep your credit utilization below 30% to demonstrate responsible credit management. Higher utilization can indicate a higher risk of defaulting on your debts. Regularly monitor your credit card balances and aim to pay them off in full each month to maintain a healthy credit utilization ratio.

Diversify Your Credit Mix:

Lenders and credit bureaus consider the types of credit you have when evaluating your creditworthiness. Having a diverse credit mix, such as a combination of credit cards, loans, and mortgages, can positively impact your credit score. However, it's essential to only take on credit that you can manage responsibly and avoid accumulating excessive debt.

Regularly Monitor Your Credit:

Stay vigilant about your credit health by regularly monitoring your credit reports and scores. You are entitled to a free credit report from each of the three major credit bureaus (Equifax, Experian, and TransUnion) once a year. Review these reports for any errors or fraudulent activities and promptly dispute any inaccuracies you find. Several online services and mobile apps also provide free credit monitoring, allowing you to track changes to your credit profile.

Be Patient and Persistent:

Building good credit takes time and consistent effort. It requires responsible financial behavior and a long-term perspective. As you establish positive credit habits and demonstrate responsible borrowing, your credit score will gradually improve. Be patient, stay committed to your financial goals, and avoid taking shortcuts that may harm your creditworthin establishing and improving your credit is a crucial aspect of achieving financial success. By understanding the basics of credit, starting with the essentials, making timely payments, keeping credit utilization low, diversifying your credit mix, regularly monitoring your credit, and exercising patience, you can build a solid credit foundation. Remember, responsible credit management is a lifelong practice that can unlock doors to better financial opportunities and empower you to reach your goals.

Monitoring and Protecting Your Credit

Your credit plays a crucial role in your financial well-being. It affects your ability to secure loans, obtain favorable interest rates, and even impacts employment opportunities. With the increasing prevalence of identity theft and data breaches, monitoring and protecting your credit has become more important than ever. In this article, we will explore the importance of monitoring your credit and provide essential tips for safeguarding your financial reputation.

Why Monitor Your Credit?

Monitoring your credit is an essential practice to stay informed about your financial standing and to detect any suspicious activity or errors that could harm your credit score. Here are some key reasons why credit monitoring is crucial:

Early Detection of Fraudulent Activity: Regularly monitoring your credit allows you to quickly identify signs of identity theft or fraudulent activity. Unauthorized credit inquiries, unfamiliar accounts, or sudden changes in your credit score can all be indicators of potential fraud.

Timely Error Correction: Mistakes can happen, and errors in your credit report could negatively impact your creditworthiness. By monitoring your credit, you can spot inaccuracies or discrepancies in your report and take immediate steps to rectify them.

Improving Credit Awareness: Monitoring your credit provides you with a comprehensive understanding of your credit behavior and financial habits. This awareness enables you to make informed decisions, manage your debt responsibly, and work towards improving your credit score over time.

Tips for Protecting Your Credit
Alongside credit monitoring, it is essential to take proactive measures to protect your credit from potential threats. Here are some practical tips to safeguard your financial reputation:

Regularly Check Your Credit Reports: Obtain free copies of your credit reports from major credit bureaus (Equifax, Experian, and TransUnion) annually. Review them carefully, looking for any errors or suspicious activity. Reporting any inaccuracies promptly is crucial for maintaining a healthy credit profile.

Set Up Fraud Alerts and Credit Freezes: Consider placing fraud alerts or credit freezes on your credit reports. A fraud alert notifies lenders to verify your identity before extending credit, while a credit freeze restricts access to your credit report altogether, making it difficult for identity thieves to open new accounts in your name.

Secure Personal and Financial Information: Safeguard your personal information by using strong, unique passwords for your financial accounts and regularly updating them. Be cautious of phishing attempts, never sharing personal details via email or phone unless you initiate the communication

Monitor Your Accounts: Regularly review your bank statements, credit card statements, and other financial accounts for any unauthorized transactions. Report suspicious activity immediately to your financial institution.

Be Wary of Public Wi-Fi: When accessing sensitive financial information or making online transactions, avoid using public Wi-Fi networks, as they can be vulnerable to hackers. Opt for secure, password-protected networks or use a virtual private network (VPN) for added security.

Monitoring and protecting your credit is a vital practice for maintaining a healthy financial profile. By staying vigilant, regularly monitoring your credit reports, and implementing protective measures, you can detect and prevent potential fraud, correct errors promptly, and take control of your financial future. Prioritizing the security of your credit ensures that you can make informed financial decisions and enjoy greater peace of mind in an increasingly digital world.

Chapter 5

Safeguarding Your Family's Financial Future

Safeguarding refers to the actions and measures taken to protect and promote the welfare of individuals, particularly vulnerable groups such as children, young people, and adults at risk. It involves the prevention and response to potential harm, abuse, or neglect, and aims to ensure that people's rights are respected and their well-being is prioritized.

In various contexts, safeguarding may have different focuses, but the underlying goal is to create safe environments and prevent harm. Some key areas where safeguarding is crucial include:

Child Safeguarding: This involves protecting children and ensuring their welfare, both in general settings and specific environments like schools, childcare facilities, and youth organizations.

Adult Safeguarding: It focuses on the well-being of vulnerable adults who may be at risk of abuse, exploitation, or neglect, such as elderly individuals, individuals with disabilities, or those with mental health issues.

Online Safeguarding: With the increasing use of digital technologies, online safeguarding aims to protect individuals from various online risks, including cyberbullying, grooming, exposure to harmful content, and online exploitation.

Organizational Safeguarding: This pertains to the policies, procedures, and practices implemented by organizations, such as schools, healthcare facilities, or community groups, to ensure the safety and well-being of the individuals they serve.

Safeguarding typically involves a range of actions, such as risk assessments, establishing safe environments, raising awareness, training staff and volunteers, implementing reporting mechanisms, and responding to concerns or allegations of abuse or neglect. It is a collective responsibility involving individuals, families, communities, organizations, and relevant authorities to create a protective and supportive environment for everyone.

Insurance and Risk Management: Safeguarding Your Future

Life is full of uncertainties, and we all face risks in various aspects of our lives. Whether it's a natural disaster, an unforeseen accident, or a sudden illness, these unexpected events can have a significant impact on our financial well-being. Insurance and risk management provide a crucial safety net that protects individuals, businesses, and communities against potential losses. In this article, we delve into the world of insurance and risk management and explore why they are essential for safeguarding our future.

Understanding Risk Management:

Risk management involves identifying, assessing, and mitigating potential risks that may affect an individual or an organization. It is a systematic approach that helps in reducing the impact of adverse events. Risk management includes analyzing potential risks, developing strategies to minimize or transfer them, and implementing preventive measures.

The Role of Insurance:

Insurance acts as a powerful tool within the framework of risk management. It is a contract between an insurer (the insurance company) and the insured (the policyholder), wherein the insurer agrees to provide financial compensation in case of a covered loss. By paying regular premiums, individuals and businesses transfer the financial burden of potential losses to the insurer, thereby reducing their exposure to risk.

Types of Insurance:

Insurance encompasses a wide range of coverage options designed to protect against specific risks. Some common types of insurance include:

Health Insurance: Provides coverage for medical expenses and treatments, offering peace of mind during times of illness or injury.

Auto Insurance: Protects against financial loss due to vehicle accidents, theft, or damage.

Homeowners/Renters Insurance: Safeguards properties against risks such as fire, theft, or natural disasters.

Life Insurance: Offers financial protection to beneficiaries in the event of the insured person's death, providing support for dependents and loved ones.

Business Insurance: Assists companies in managing risks related to liability, property damage, employee injuries, and other business-specific concerns.

Risk Management Strategies:
Effective risk management involves implementing various strategies to minimize and control potential risks. These strategies may include:

Risk Avoidance: Completely eliminating activities or situations that carry substantial risks.

Risk Reduction: Implementing measures to reduce the probability or impact of a risk. For example, installing security systems to minimize the risk of theft.

Risk Transfer: Shifting the financial burden of potential losses to an insurance company by purchasing insurance policies.

Risk Retention: Accepting a certain level of risk and self-insuring by setting aside funds to cover potential losses.

Benefits of Insurance and Risk Management:
Financial Protection: Insurance provides a safety net that shields individuals and businesses from significant financial losses. It ensures that individuals and their families can maintain their quality of life during difficult times.

Business Continuity: For businesses, insurance and risk management strategies help in minimizing disruptions and ensuring continuity of operations in the face of unexpected events.

Peace of Mind: Knowing that you are adequately protected against potential risks brings peace of mind. It allows individuals and businesses to focus on their goals and objectives without constant worry about unforeseen circumstances.

Insurance and risk management are indispensable components of financial planning. They provide a vital layer of protection against uncertainties, enabling individuals and businesses to navigate through challenging situations with confidence. By understanding the risks we face and implementing appropriate risk management strategies, we can safeguard our future and secure a more resilient tomorrow.

Types of Insurance Coverage for Families
Families have various insurance coverage options to protect themselves and their loved ones. Here are some common types of insurance coverage that families often consider:

Health Insurance: Health insurance provides coverage for medical expenses, including doctor visits, hospitalization, medications, and surgeries. It helps families pay for healthcare services and protects against high medical costs.

Life Insurance: Life insurance provides financial protection to the family in case of the insured person's death. It pays a lump sum or regular payments to the beneficiaries, helping cover expenses such as funeral costs, mortgage payments, and future financial needs.

Homeowners/Renters Insurance: Homeowners insurance protects homeowners against damages or losses to their property, including the dwelling, personal belongings, and liability for accidents. Renters insurance provides similar coverage for tenants, protecting their personal belongings and providing liability coverage.

Auto Insurance: Auto insurance covers damages or injuries resulting from car accidents. It typically includes liability coverage (for damages caused to others), collision coverage (for damage to your vehicle), and comprehensive coverage (for non-collision incidents like theft or natural disasters).

Disability Insurance: Disability insurance offers income protection in case the insured person becomes unable to work due to an illness or injury. It replaces a portion of lost income, helping families meet their financial obligations during the disability period.

Umbrella Insurance: Umbrella insurance provides additional liability coverage beyond the limits of other primary policies, such as homeowners or auto insurance. It offers protection against significant claims or lawsuits that exceed the standard policy limits.

Dental Insurance: Dental insurance covers a portion of dental care expenses, including routine check-ups, cleanings, and dental procedures. It helps families maintain good oral health and manage dental treatment costs.

Vision Insurance: Vision insurance assists with the costs of eye exams, prescription eyewear (glasses or contact lenses), and other vision-related services. It helps families access necessary vision care and maintain good eye health.

Long-Term Care Insurance: Long-term care insurance provides coverage for long-term care services, such as nursing home care, assisted living facilities, or in-home care. It helps families manage the high costs of long-term care for aging or disabled family members.

Critical Illness Insurance: Critical illness insurance pays a lump sum or regular payments if the insured person is diagnosed with a specified critical illness, such as cancer, heart attack, or stroke. It helps families manage medical expenses and financial burdens during challenging times.

It's essential to review your specific needs and consult with insurance professionals to determine which types of coverage are most appropriate for your family's circumstances.

Making Informed Insurance Decisions
Making informed insurance decisions is crucial when it comes to protecting yourself, your assets, and your financial well-being. Insurance provides a safety net against unexpected events and risks, but choosing the right coverage requires careful consideration and understanding. Here are a few key points to keep in mind when making informed insurance decisions:

Assess your needs: Begin by evaluating your specific insurance needs. Consider your personal circumstances, such as your age, health, family situation, and financial goals. Identify the risks you face and determine the types of insurance that can mitigate those risks effectively.

Research and compare: Take the time to research different insurance providers, policies, and coverage options. Compare premiums, deductibles, coverage limits, and exclusions. Look for reputable companies with a good track record and positive customer reviews.

Understand policy terms: Carefully read and understand the terms and conditions of the insurance policies you are considering. Pay attention to the coverage details, limitations, and any exclusions that may apply. If there are terms or concepts you don't understand, reach out to the insurance provider or seek professional advice.

Seek professional advice: If you find insurance jargon confusing or if you're unsure about certain aspects of a policy, consult with an insurance agent or broker. These professionals can provide guidance, explain complex terms, and help you navigate the insurance landscape to make well-informed decisions.

Consider affordability: While it's important to have adequate coverage, it's also crucial to consider your budget. Determine how much you can comfortably afford to pay for insurance premiums without compromising your financial stability. Balance the level of coverage you need with the cost of the premiums.

Review and update regularly: Insurance needs can change over time due to various factors such as lifestyle changes, acquiring new assets, or reaching different life stages. Review your insurance coverage periodically to ensure it aligns with your current needs and make necessary adjustments if required.

Evaluate customer service: Apart from the policy features and costs, consider the customer service provided by insurance companies. Look for insurers with a reputation for responsive and reliable customer support. Prompt and efficient claims processing is also an essential aspect to consider.

Seek recommendations and referrals: Talk to friends, family, or colleagues who have experience with the insurance providers or policies you are considering. Their firsthand experiences can provide valuable insights and help you make a more informed decision.

By following these steps and taking the time to research, understand, and compare insurance options, you can make informed decisions that align with your specific needs and financial goals. Remember, insurance is a long-term commitment, and making the right choices can provide you with peace of mind and financial protection in times of uncertainty.

Chapter 6

Teaching Delayed Gratification

Delayed gratification refers to the ability to resist the temptation of an immediate reward in favor of obtaining a more substantial or long-term reward in the future. It involves exhibiting self-control, patience, and the willingness to tolerate a certain amount of discomfort or delay in order to achieve a desired outcome.

The concept of delayed gratification gained prominence through the Stanford marshmallow experiment conducted in the late 1960s and early 1970s. In this experiment, young children were given the choice to either eat one marshmallow immediately or wait for a short period, typically 15 minutes, and receive two marshmallows as a reward. The study found that children who were able to delay gratification and wait for the larger reward tended to exhibit more positive life outcomes, such as better academic performance, higher SAT scores, and better social skills.

Delayed gratification is a crucial skill for achieving long-term goals and success in various areas of life, including education, career, finances, health, and relationships. It involves sacrificing immediate pleasure or instant gratification in order to reap greater rewards in the future. By delaying gratification, individuals can develop discipline, build resilience, and make choices that align with their long-term objectives.

Practicing delayed gratification can be challenging, especially in a society that often promotes instant gratification through various means like fast food, online shopping, or social media. However, cultivating this skill can lead to greater self-control, improved decision-making, and a stronger ability to achieve personal goals.

significance in achieving long-term financial goals.

In today's fast-paced world, setting and achieving long-term financial goals is crucial for securing a stable and prosperous future. Whether it's saving for retirement, purchasing a home, or funding your child's education, having a clear vision and diligently working towards these objectives can pave the way for financial security and peace of mind. In this article, we will explore the significance of achieving long-term financial goals and how they can positively impact our lives.

Financial Stability and Independence

One of the primary benefits of setting and achieving long-term financial goals is attaining stability and independence. When you have a plan in place and actively work towards it, you gain control over your finances. This control empowers you to make informed decisions, such as managing debt, building an emergency fund, and making wise investments. By attaining financial stability, you reduce the stress associated with money-related uncertainties and gain the freedom to live life on your own terms.

Retirement Planning and Security
Retirement planning is a critical long-term financial goal that requires careful consideration and early action. By envisioning your retirement lifestyle and setting financial targets accordingly, you can ensure a comfortable and worry-free future. Accumulating savings, investing wisely, and taking advantage of retirement vehicles like pension plans or individual retirement accounts (IRAs) are all crucial steps towards achieving long-term financial security. The sooner you start, the greater the potential for your investments to grow, enabling you to maintain your desired standard of living during retirement.

Personal and Professional Aspirations

Long-term financial goals not only provide a sense of security but also pave the way for pursuing personal and professional aspirations. For example, saving for higher education can open doors to better career opportunities and increased earning potential. Similarly, saving for a down payment on a home enables you to establish stability and potentially build equity. Achieving these goals can unlock new possibilities and enhance your overall quality of life, giving you the freedom to explore your passions and interests.

Creating a Legacy

Beyond personal benefits, achieving long-term financial goals allows you to create a lasting legacy. By planning your estate and ensuring the seamless transfer of wealth to future generations, you can protect and preserve your hard-earned assets. Setting up a will, establishing trusts, and engaging in tax-efficient strategies can help ensure your loved ones are taken care of, while also supporting charitable causes that align with your values. This sense of purpose and the ability to positively impact future generations can be incredibly rewarding.

Peace of Mind and Reduced Financial Stress
Lastly, achieving long-term financial goals provides a profound sense of peace of mind. By taking control of your financial future, you reduce anxiety and stress associated with money-related concerns. The knowledge that you are actively working towards a secure future allows you to focus on other aspects of your life, such as family, relationships, and personal growth. Financial stability acts as a strong foundation, enabling you to weather unexpected challenges and take advantage of new opportunities without being overwhelmed by financial worries.

The significance of achieving long-term financial goals cannot be overstated. By setting clear objectives and diligently working towards them, you can attain financial stability, independence, and peace of mind. Whether it's planning for retirement, funding education, or building wealth, long-term financial goals provide direction and purpose in our lives. Start today, make a plan, and take small steps each day towards securing your financial future. The rewards will be worth the effort as you build a solid foundation for a prosperous and fulfilling life.

Chapter 7

Retirement and planning

Retirement is a significant milestone in our lives, marking the beginning of a new chapter filled with leisure, personal pursuits, and quality time with loved ones. However, the journey to a comfortable and fulfilling retirement requires careful planning, especially when it comes to starting early. In this article, we will explore the importance of early retirement planning and why taking proactive steps towards securing your financial future is crucial.

Building Sufficient Savings

One of the primary reasons for early retirement planning is to build a sufficient nest egg to support your desired lifestyle during retirement. Starting early allows you to benefit from the power of compounding, where your investments generate returns over time, leading to substantial growth. By starting early, even modest contributions can accumulate into a sizable retirement fund, providing financial security and peace of mind in your later years.

Addressing Potential Challenges

Retirement planning is not just about accumulating wealth; it also involves considering potential challenges and devising strategies to overcome them. By starting early, you have a longer timeframe to address factors such as inflation, rising healthcare costs, and unpredictable economic conditions. Planning for these contingencies early on enables you to make adjustments, diversify your investments, and seek professional advice when needed, ensuring a robust and resilient retirement plan.

Maximizing Retirement Account Benefits

Many countries offer retirement savings accounts with tax advantages, such as 401(k)s or Individual Retirement Accounts (IRAs). By beginning your retirement planning early, you can take full advantage of these tax-efficient accounts and benefit from employer-matching contributions. Moreover, some retirement plans have annual contribution limits, so starting early allows you to contribute consistently over a longer period, potentially reaching the maximum allowable amount and maximizing your retirement savings.

Flexibility and Freedom of Choice

Early retirement planning provides you with flexibility and the freedom to choose how and when you retire. It allows you to set realistic goals and determine the lifestyle you aspire to achieve during your golden years. By developing a well-thought-out plan and diligently saving early, you can work towards retiring at an age that aligns with your aspirations, whether it's traveling the world, pursuing a passion project, or spending quality time with your family.

Peace of Mind and Reduced Stress

Financial worries can be a significant source of stress, particularly as retirement approaches. Early retirement planning helps alleviate this stress by providing you with a roadmap for your financial future. By having a comprehensive plan in place, you can better manage your finances, monitor your progress, and make any necessary adjustments along the way. This peace of mind allows you to focus on enjoying your retirement years rather than being burdened by financial concerns.

Retirement Accounts and Investments.

Retirement is a significant milestone in one's life, marking the transition from a career-oriented phase to a time of relaxation and personal fulfillment. To ensure financial stability during this period, it is essential to make wise investment decisions and take advantage of retirement accounts. In this article, we will explore the world of retirement accounts and investments, offering guidance on how to build a secure future.

Understanding Retirement Accounts

Retirement accounts are financial vehicles specifically designed to help individuals save for retirement and enjoy tax advantages along the way. Here are a few common types:

a) 401(k) Plans: Offered by employers, these employer-sponsored plans allow employees to contribute a portion of their salary, often with an employer match. Contributions are made pre-tax, and the funds grow tax-deferred until retirement.

b) Individual Retirement Accounts (IRAs): IRAs are personal retirement accounts that individuals can open independently. Traditional IRAs offer tax-deferred growth, while Roth IRAs provide tax-free withdrawals in retirement.

c) Simplified Employee Pension (SEP) IRA: Designed for self-employed individuals and small business owners, SEP IRAs offer higher contribution limits and tax advantages similar to traditional IRAs.

Importance of Diversification
Diversification is a key principle of successful investing, and it becomes even more crucial when planning for retirement. By spreading your investments across different asset classes, such as stocks, bonds, and real estate, you can reduce risk and enhance potential returns. A well-diversified portfolio can help protect your retirement savings from the volatility of any single investment.

Balancing Risk and Return

Retirement investing requires striking a balance between risk and return. Generally, the younger you are, the more risk you can afford to take as you have more time to recover from potential losses. As you approach retirement, it is prudent to gradually shift towards more conservative investments to preserve capital. Consulting with a financial advisor can help determine the appropriate asset allocation based on your risk tolerance and retirement goals.

Tax Advantages of Retirement Accounts

One of the significant benefits of retirement accounts is their tax advantages. Contributions to traditional retirement accounts are made with pre-tax dollars, reducing your taxable income in the year of contribution. Additionally, these accounts grow tax-deferred, meaning you don't pay taxes on investment gains until you withdraw funds in retirement.

Roth retirement accounts, on the other hand, offer tax-free withdrawals in retirement. While contributions are made with after-tax dollars, all qualified withdrawals, including earnings, are tax-free. Roth accounts can be an excellent option for those who anticipate being in a higher tax bracket during retirement.

Maximizing Employer Contributions

If your employer offers a retirement plan, such as a 401(k), it is crucial to take full advantage of any matching contributions they provide. Employer matches are essentially free money that can significantly boost your retirement savings. Strive to contribute at least enough to receive the maximum matching contribution to capitalize on this valuable benefit.

Regular Monitoring and Rebalancing

Retirement planning is not a one-time event but an ongoing process. Regularly monitor your investment performance and make necessary adjustments to ensure your portfolio remains aligned with your goals. Rebalancing involves periodically realigning your asset allocation to maintain the desired risk profile. It is advisable to review your retirement accounts and investments annually or seek professional advice to optimize your strategy

Retirement accounts and investments play a crucial role in securing a comfortable future. By understanding the various retirement account options, diversifying your investments, balancing risk and return, and taking advantage of tax benefits, you can build a robust retirement portfolio. Regular monitoring and maximizing employer contributions further contribute to a financially secure retirement. Remember, starting early and seeking professional advice when needed are key steps toward achieving your retirement goals.

Strategies for Maximizing Retirement Savings

Start saving early:

The power of compound interest cannot be overstated when it comes to retirement savings. The earlier you begin saving, the longer your money has to grow. Even small contributions made over an extended period can accumulate significantly over time. Make it a priority to allocate a portion of your income towards retirement savings as soon as you enter the workforce.

Take full advantage of employer-sponsored plans:

If your employer offers a retirement savings plan such as a 401(k) or a similar option, contribute as much as you can, especially if there is an employer match. Employer matches represent free money and can significantly boost your savings. Aim to contribute at least enough to receive the full employer match to maximize your benefits.

Diversify your investments:

Diversification is a key principle in investing, especially when it comes to retirement savings. Allocate your funds across different asset classes such as stocks, bonds, and real estate to spread out the risk. Diversification can help protect your savings from the volatility of any particular investment and increase the likelihood of long-term growth.

Increase contributions over time:

As your income grows, consider increasing your retirement contributions. Each time you receive a raise or a bonus, allocate a portion of that additional income towards your retirement savings. Gradually increasing your contributions allows you to benefit from compounding while adjusting to changes in your financial situation.

Reduce expenses and live within your means:

Cutting back on unnecessary expenses and living within your means frees up additional funds that can be directed towards retirement savings. Evaluate your budget and identify areas where you can make cost-saving adjustments. Small lifestyle changes, such as eating out less frequently or canceling unused subscriptions, can make a significant difference in the long run.

Consider catch-up contributions:

If you're over the age of 50, take advantage of catch-up contributions allowed by retirement plans. These additional contributions are designed to help individuals "catch up" on their savings if they started saving later in life. Catch-up contributions can help accelerate your retirement savings growth and bridge the gap between your current savings and your desired retirement fund.

Regularly review and rebalance your portfolio:
It's essential to review your investment portfolio periodically to ensure it aligns with your retirement goals and risk tolerance. As you approach retirement, consider adjusting your asset allocation to reduce risk and protect your accumulated savings. Consult with a financial advisor who can provide guidance based on your specific needs and circumstances.

Chapter 8

Teaching children about money

Kid's Financial Education

In today's complex and ever-changing world, it is essential to equip children with the necessary knowledge and skills to make sound financial decisions from an early age. Age-appropriate financial education plays a crucial role in empowering children to develop healthy money habits, understand the value of money, and become financially responsible individuals in the future.

Starting financial education at a young age allows children to develop a strong foundation of financial literacy and gradually build upon it as they grow older. The key is to tailor the education to their developmental stage and make it engaging, practical, and relatable. Here are some key points to consider when providing age-appropriate financial education for kids:

Early Years (Ages 3-6): At this stage, the focus should be on introducing basic concepts related to money, such as recognizing coins and bills, understanding their values, and distinguishing between needs and wants. Through simple activities, such as playing pretend stores or using piggy banks, children can begin to grasp the idea of saving and spending.

Elementary School (Ages 7-12): As children progress into elementary school, financial education can become more comprehensive. They can learn about budgeting, setting savings goals, and the importance of making informed choices. Interactive games, such as creating a budget for a virtual pet or managing a mock business, can make these concepts more enjoyable and practical.

Teenage Years (Ages 13-18): During adolescence, financial education should focus on more advanced topics, including understanding credit, debt management, and long-term financial planning. Teaching teenagers about the value of saving for future goals, such as college or a car, and introducing basic investing concepts can set them on a path to financial independence and success.

Practical Application: It's crucial to provide children with real-world opportunities to apply their financial knowledge. Encourage them to earn money through chores or part-time jobs, and guide them in budgeting and saving for desired purchases. Involve them in family financial discussions to foster an understanding of budgeting, bills, and responsible spending.

Continual Learning: Financial education should be an ongoing process. Encourage children to read books or articles about personal finance, participate in workshops or camps focused on money management, and explore online resources specifically designed for their age group. Reinforcing financial knowledge throughout their education will help them make informed financial decisions as adults.

By instilling age-appropriate financial education, we can equip children with essential skills that will serve them well throughout their lives. Teaching them the value of money, budgeting, saving, and responsible spending will contribute to their financial well-being and empower them to navigate the complex world of personal finance confidently.

Developing Healthy Money Habits in Children
In an increasingly complex and financially driven world, it is vital to equip our children with the tools and knowledge to navigate the realm of personal finance. By instilling healthy money habits from an early age, we empower our children to make responsible financial decisions, cultivate savings, and build a strong foundation for their future. In

this article, we will explore some effective strategies for developing healthy money habits in children.

Lead by Example:
Children often learn best through observation and emulation. As parents or guardians, it is crucial to model healthy money habits ourselves. Demonstrating responsible spending, budgeting, saving, and charitable giving can have a profound impact on our children's financial mindset. By displaying positive money behaviors, we set the stage for them to develop similar habits.

Introduce Basic Concepts:
Introducing basic financial concepts to children at an appropriate age helps demystify money and its role in their lives. Engage in age-appropriate discussions about needs versus wants, the importance of saving, and the concept of budgeting. Simple activities such as playing store or

setting up a pretend bank can provide hands-on experiences that make financial concepts tangible and relatable.

Encourage Saving:
Encouraging children to save fosters discipline and delayed gratification. Provide them with piggy banks or saving jars and explain the benefits of setting money aside for future needs or goals. Help them establish short-term and long-term saving targets, such as purchasing a toy or saving for a college fund. Offering incentives or matching their savings contributions can also motivate them to develop a regular saving habit.

Allow Financial Decision-Making:
Granting children some financial autonomy allows them to learn from their choices and understand the consequences of their actions. Start by giving them a small allowance and allowing them to make decisions about how to spend or save it. As they

grow older, involve them in family budgeting discussions and decision-making, such as planning for vacations or setting financial goals. This involvement cultivates a sense of responsibility and ownership over money matters.

Teach the Value of Work:
Teaching children the value of hard work and the connection between effort and earning can be invaluable. Encourage them to engage in age-appropriate chores or tasks around the house for which they can earn an allowance. This instills a sense of responsibility, work ethic, and understanding that money is earned through effort. Additionally, discussing various careers and the importance of education can inspire them to set long-term goals and understand the connection between education, career, and financial stability.

Practice Philanthropy:
Help children develop empathy and generosity by introducing them to the concept of philanthropy. Encourage them to donate a portion of their savings to causes they care about. Engage in volunteer activities as a family, emphasizing the value of giving back to the community. These experiences foster a sense of gratitude, social responsibility, and the understanding that money can be used to make a positive impact on others' lives.

Emphasize Smart Spending:
Teach children to differentiate between needs and wants, and the importance of making informed purchasing decisions. Encourage them to compare prices, read reviews, and evaluate alternatives before making a purchase. Introduce the concept of delayed gratification by discussing the benefits of saving up for a higher-quality item rather than making impulsive purchases. This cultivates critical

thinking skills and helps them become mindful consumers.

Developing healthy money habits in children is an investment in their future well-being. By leading by example, introducing basic financial concepts, encouraging saving, allowing financial decision-making, teaching the value of work, practicing philanthropy, and emphasizing smart spending, we equip our children with the essential skills they need to become financially responsible adults. By instilling these habits early on, we empower them to navigate the complex financial landscape, make informed decisions, and achieve long-term financial stability.

Teaching Money Management Skills
Money management is a crucial life skill that everyone needs to navigate the complexities of personal finances. By starting early, parents and educators can empower children with the necessary tools and knowledge to make informed financial

decisions. Teaching children about money management not only cultivates responsible spending habits but also lays the foundation for long-term financial success. Here are some key strategies to effectively teach money management skills to children.

Start young: Introducing money concepts to children at a young age helps them develop a basic understanding of its value. Begin by teaching them the different denominations and their corresponding values. As they grow older, introduce concepts like saving, budgeting, and the importance of delayed gratification.

Make it practical: Encourage hands-on learning experiences that allow children to apply money management skills in real-life situations. For example, give them an allowance and guide them on how to divide it into spending, saving, and sharing categories. This exercise teaches them the importance of budgeting and setting financial goals. Lead by example: Children observe and learn from the behavior of their parents and guardians. Demonstrate responsible financial habits by involving them in discussions about household budgeting, saving for specific goals, and making wise spending choices. Show them how to differentiate between needs and wants, and the importance of saving for the future.

Teach them the value of money: Help children understand the effort and hard work required to earn money. Encourage them to take on age-appropriate chores or offer opportunities for them to earn money through entrepreneurial endeavors, such as selling homemade crafts or providing services like pet sitting. This helps instill a sense of responsibility and a work ethic.

Set savings goals: Teach children the importance of saving by setting achievable savings goals. Whether it's for a toy they desire or a larger purchase, encourage them to save a portion of their allowance or earnings regularly. Help them track their progress and celebrate milestones along the way, fostering a sense of accomplishment and discipline.

Introduce banking concepts: As children grow older, introduce them to banking concepts such as savings accounts. Take them to a bank or credit union to open a savings account in their name. Teach them about interest, deposits, withdrawals, and the importance of maintaining a healthy balance.

Emphasize wise spending choices: Teach children to think critically about their spending decisions. Encourage them to compare prices, read product reviews, and consider the value and durability of the items they wish to purchase. This helps them develop a habit of making informed choices and avoiding impulsive purchases.

Teach the concept of debt: As children mature, introduce the concept of borrowing and debt. Explain how credit cards work, emphasizing the importance of responsible credit card usage and timely repayment. Highlight the potential consequences of excessive debt, such as high interest rates and financial stress.

Foster an entrepreneurial spirit: Encourage children to explore their entrepreneurial side by starting small businesses or participating in fundraising activities. This helps them develop skills such as money management, marketing, customer service, and problem-solving, while also instilling an entrepreneurial mindset.

Incorporate financial education: Utilize age-appropriate books, games, and online resources to supplement their financial education. Many educational programs and websites offer interactive tools and resources designed specifically for children to learn about money management in a fun and engaging way.

By teaching children money management skills, we equip them with the tools they need to make responsible financial decisions throughout their lives. These skills foster independence, discipline, and an understanding of the value of money. With a solid foundation in money management, children are better prepared to navigate the complexities of personal finance and achieve long-term financial success.